A Benjamin Blog
and his Inquisitive Dog
Investigation

Exploring Coasts

Anita Ganeri

Heinemann
LIBRARY

Chicago, Illinois

© 2014 Heinemann Library
an imprint of Capstone Global Library, LLC
Chicago, Illinois

To contact Capstone Global Library please
phone 800-747-4992, or visit our web site,
www.capstonepub.com

Edited by Dan Nunn, Rebecca Rissman, and Helen
Cox Cannons
Designed by Joanna Hinton-Malivoire
Original illustrations © Capstone Global Library Ltd
Illustrated by Sernur ISIK
Picture research by Mica Brancic
Production by Helen McCreath
Originated by Capstone Global Library Ltd
Printed and bound in China

17 16 15 14 13
10 9 8 7 6 5 4 3 2 1

**Library of Congress Cataloging-in-Publication
Data**
Ganeri, Anita, 1961- author.
  Exploring coasts : a Benjamin Blog and his
inquisitive dog investigation / Anita Ganeri.
    pages cm.—(Exploring habitats, with Benjamin
Blog and his inquisitive dog)
  Includes bibliographical references and index.
  ISBN 978-1-4329-8777-0 (hb)—ISBN 978-1-4329-
8784-8 (pb) 1. Coastal ecology—Juvenile literature.
2. Coasts—Juvenile literature. 3. Coastal animals—
Juvenile literature. I. Title.

QH541.5.C65G36 2014
551.45'7—dc23   2013017414

Acknowledgments
The author and publisher are grateful to the
following for permission to reproduce copyright
material: Getty Images pp. 14 (E+/stockcam); 15
(© LRM Photography), 26 (Universal ImagesGroup);
Photoshot p. 16 (© NHPA/Laurie Campbell);
Shutterstock pp. 4 (© Mariusz S. Jurgielewicz),
6 (© Elena Elisseeva), 7 (© Galyna Andrushko),
9 (© Pavelk), 10 (© Richard Cavalleri), 11 (©
alexmcguffie), 12 (© Robyn Mackenzie), 13 (©
Liliya Krasnova), 17 (© Karin Wassmer), 18 (© Julian
Weber), 19 (© LiteChoices), 20 (© Natursports),
21 (© David Evison), 22 (© Ignacio Salaverria),
24 (© Oliver Hoffmann), 25 (© David Young), 27
(© Sergei Butorin), 29 bottom (© David Young),
29 top (© Stanislav Komogorov); SuperStock pp.
5 (All Canada Photos/Darwin Wiggett), 8 (Robert
Harding Picture Library), 23 (F1 ONLINE).

Cover photograph of the Twelve Apostles in
Victoria, Australia, reproduced with permission of
Shutterstock (© Ashley Whitworth).

We would like to thank Michael Bright for his
invaluable help in the preparation of this book.

Every effort has been made to contact copyright
holders of any material reproduced in this book.
Any omissions will be rectified in subsequent
printings if notice is given to the publisher.

All the Internet addresses (URLs) given in this
book were valid at the time of going to press.
However, due to the dynamic nature of the
Internet, some addresses may have changed,
or sites may have changed or ceased to exist
since publication. While the author and publisher
regret any inconvenience this may cause readers,
no responsibility for any such changes can be
accepted by either the author or the publisher.

Some words are shown in bold, **like this**. You can find
out what they mean by looking in the glossary.

Contents

Welcome to the Coast!

Hello! My name's Benjamin Blog and this is Barko Polo, my **inquisitive** dog. (He's named after the ancient ace explorer **Marco Polo**.) We have just returned from our latest adventure— exploring coasts around the world. We put this book together from some of the blog posts we wrote on the way.

BARKO'S BLOG-TASTIC COAST FACTS

Coasts are places where the land meets the ocean. Canada has the longest coast of any country at 125,566 miles (202,080 kilometers). If you straightened it out, it would reach five times around the **equator**.

Changing Tides

Posted by: Ben Blog | March 2 at 11:15 a.m.

Every day, the coast changes because of the **tides**. Twice a day, at high tide, the ocean floods onto the shore. Twice a day, at low tide, it flows back out again. I'm in Brittany, France, at low tide—a great time to explore the beach. At high tide, the water can easily cut you off from the land.

The ocean never stays still. Waves are huge ripples of water that the wind whips up as it blows across the ocean. When the waves crash onto the shore, this is called breaking.

By the Seashore

Posted by: Ben Blog | April 23 at 12:14 p.m.

We arrived on the island of Hawaii, in the Pacific Ocean, and headed straight for the beach. It's covered in strange black sand that's made from crushed-up rocks from volcanoes. Sand is made when the wind and waves smash rocks, shells, and **coral** into tiny pieces.

BARKO'S BLOG-TASTIC COAST FACTS
Have you ever collected pebbles on a beach? They are often round and smooth. That is because they are rubbed and scraped against each other by the power of the waves.

Caves, Stacks, and Arches

Posted by: Ben Blog | June 28 at 1:31 p.m.

From Hawaii, we headed to South Africa and the Cape of Good Hope. The cape is a **headland**—a rocky piece of land sticking out into the ocean. It's been worn into this shape by the wind and waves. The wind and waves also carve out features along the coast, such as caves, **stacks**, and **arches**.

BARKO'S BLOG-TASTIC COAST FACTS

When waves wear away at cracks in a headland, they carve out ocean caves. Fingal's Cave on the coast of the island of Staffa, Scotland, is named after a giant in Scottish legend. Yikes!

The next stop was Australia, to explore the Twelve Apostles. Here's one of the photos I took. These amazing rocks are ocean stacks, and some of them are as tall as four houses. An ocean stack forms when the top of an arch collapses, leaving behind a tall pillar of rock.

BARKO'S BLOG-TASTIC COAST FACTS

This stunning arch is on the island of Gozo in the Mediterranean Sea. It was made when the ocean wore a hole between two caves on either side of the headland.

Cliff Climber

Posted by: Ben Blog | July 7 at 11:11 a.m.

Cliffs are steep walls of rock that plunge into the ocean along coasts. These are the White Cliffs of Dover in England. They are white because they are made from **chalk**. They have been carved into shape by the wind and waves. I went climbing to get a better look.

I am here.

BARKO'S BLOG-TASTIC COAST FACTS

The highest ocean cliffs in the world are back in Hawaii. To reach the lookout at the top, you need to climb for more than ¾ mile (1 kilometer). But there is a fantastic view at the top!

Blooming Coasts

Posted by: Ben Blog | August 31 at 3:52 p.m.

It's tough being a seashore plant! At high tide, plants get covered in water. At low tide, they are left high and dry. Seaweeds, like this kelp that I took a photo of, have root-like **holdfasts** for sticking onto rocks so that they do not get washed away as the tides go in and out.

BARKO'S BLOG-TASTIC COAST FACTS

Mangrove trees grow along the coast where rivers flow into the ocean. They have special roots that stick out from their trunks. These keep the trees firmly fixed in the mud.

I spotted some clumps of this plant as I was climbing up a sand dune on the beach. It's marram grass, and you can't miss its spiky, green leaves. Its extra-long roots creep deep under the sand. They hold the plant in place, and they also stop the sand from blowing away.

BARKO'S BLOG-TASTIC COAST FACTS

Coconuts that fall from trees often drift far out to the ocean. They bob along on the water until they are washed up on another beach. There, they take root and grow into coconut palm trees.

Wet and Dry Wildlife

Posted by: Ben Blog | October 2 at 1:29 p.m.

We're on the Galapagos Islands.
I took a photo of this marine iguana.
Marine iguanas are the only lizards
that live in the ocean and on land.
They feed on seaweed that grows
on the slippery rocks. Luckily, these
iguanas are strong swimmers and
have long, sharp claws for holding on.

BARKO'S BLOG-TASTIC COAST FACTS

Sea turtles live in the ocean but come ashore to **breed**. Females dig holes in the sand and lay up to 200 eggs. When the tiny babies hatch, they head to the ocean. Many are eaten by crabs and birds.

Our next stop was the Skeleton Coast in Namibia. It's a wonderful place for spotting Cape fur seals. Tens of thousands of seals breed here in November. Visitors can view the mothers and pups from a walkway. But you don't want to get too close—the seals smell terrible!

BARKO'S BLOG-TASTIC COAST FACTS
Oystercatchers eat shellfish, such as limpets, mussels, and cockles. They use their long, pointed beaks to **lever** the shells open and get to the tasty snacks inside.

Rock Pool Life

Posted by: Ben Blog | December 19 at 2:00 p.m.

Rock pools are home to some amazing animals and are great places to explore. Sea anemones look like blobs of jelly. When the **tide** comes in, they wave their **tentacles** in the water to catch small creatures to eat. When the tide goes out, they pull them back in again.

24

BARKO'S BLOG-TASTIC COAST FACTS

Limpets cling onto the rocks with their large, sucker-like feet. This stops them from being washed away. For a better grip, they scrape a little dip in the rock to sit in.

Cracking Up

Posted by: Ben Blog | February 28 at 1:48 p.m.

In many places, coasts are in danger. Here in Holderness, in England, I'll need to watch my step. Each year, two million tons of rock from these cliffs crumble into the ocean, taking people's cliff-top homes over the edge with them.

BARKO'S BLOG-TASTIC COAST FACTS

Coasts are fantastic places to go on vacation, but large stretches have been destroyed to make space for hotels, tourist **resorts**, and golf courses. Some coasts are now **protected**.

Crooked Coasts Quiz

If you are planning your expedition along the coast, you need to be prepared. Find out how much you know about crooked coasts with our quick quiz.

1. Which country has the longest coast?
a) Namibia
b) Canada
c) South Africa

2. What is black sand made from?
a) rock from volcanoes
b) crushed-up **coral**
c) smashed seashells

3. What are the Twelve Apostles?
a) sea caves
b) sea **arches**
c) sea **stacks**

4. How do seaweeds cling to rocks?
a) with **holdfasts**
b) with anchors
c) with suckers

5. Which lizards live in the ocean?
a) chameleons
b) geckos
c) marine iguanas

6. How do sea anemones catch their food?
a) with their teeth
b) with their **tentacles**
c) with knives and forks

7. What is this?

8. What is this?

29

Glossary

arch feature along the coast made when the ocean wears a hole between two caves

breed to reproduce, or have babies

chalk soft, white rock

coral rock-like material made by tiny sea creatures

equator imaginary line that runs around the middle of Earth

headland rocky piece of land sticking out into the ocean

holdfast root-like part that fixes seaweeds to rocks

inquisitive interested in learning about the world

lever pull apart with some effort

Marco Polo explorer who lived from about 1254 to 1324. He traveled from Italy to China.

protected saved from harm or damage

resort place where people go on vacation

stack feature along the coast made when the top of an arch collapses

tentacle long, waving body part that some sea creatures use to catch food

tide how the ocean flows onto the shore and out again, twice a day

Find Out More

Books

Ganeri, Anita. *Cliff Climbers*. Chicago: Raintree, 2012.

Green, Jen. *Coasts* (Geography Wise). New York: Rosen, 2011.

Llewellyn, Claire. *Oceans* (Habitat Survival). Chicago: Raintree, 2013.

Murphy, Julie. *Ocean Animal Adaptations*. Mankato, Minn.: Capstone, 2012.

Web Sites

FactHound offers a safe, fun way to find Internet sites related to this book. All of the sites on FactHound have been researched by our staff.

Here's all you do:
Visit www.facthound.com
Type in this code: 9781432987770

Index